# ALBI CATHEDRAL
# AND BRITISH CHURCH ARCHITECTURE

# ALBI CATHEDRAL
## *and* British Church Architecture

*The influence of thirteenth-century church building
in southern France and northern Spain
upon ecclesiastical design
in modern Britain*

JOHN THOMAS

THE ECCLESIOLOGICAL SOCIETY • 2002

*For Adrian Yardley*

First published 2002

The Ecclesiological Society,
c/o Society of Antiquaries of London,
Burlington House, Piccadilly,
London WIV OHS
www.ecclsoc.org

Printed in the UK
by Pennine Printing Services Ltd,
Ripponden, West Yorkshire

ISBN 0 946823 13 8

# Contents

# Figures

## List of figures

# Preface

Architects of the later-nineteenth and early-twentieth centuries were able to draw on a vast body of historic and recent precedent in designing buildings which they considered appropriate for the needs of their day, and yet were created out of ongoing historical traditions. Their use of precedent, in many cases, was original, imaginative and varied, rather than pedestrian and repetitive.

Perhaps no better example of this exists than the way British church architects drew on Albi Cathedral and various church building methods and traditions in southern France and northern Spain, of the late-twelfth, thirteenth and early-fourteenth centuries. The fascinating aspect of the influence of Albi, in modern times, is that it affected church builders and buildings in many different ways, at different times. This study is intended to draw out the range of influences of this seminal building.

—◦◦◦—

I should like to thank: Margaret Richardson (who originally suggested this subject of study to me, and also provided additional information), and: Louise Campbell, Richard Gilbert Scott, Simon Houfe, Mary Kirk, Stan Lody, George McHardy, Anthony Quiney, Katherine Shonfield, Chris Pickford, Andor Gomme, Geoffrey Brandwood, Ken Murta, Trevor Cooper, Adrian Yardley, and Lynne Walker; they gave me much needed additional information and advice, use of the results of their unpublished research, and illustrations and photographic services, etc., etc. My research for the Appendix was greatly assisted by: Mr and Mrs Richard

Gilbert Scott, Canon E. McBride, Revd Michael Edwards, Jean Kennedy, Revd John Hawkins, Jane Kennedy, and Dr John Maddison; I would particularly thank Fr Peter Cansdale, for his assistance, hospitality and kindness, during a period of considerable personal difficulty.

Acknowledgement of reproduction copyright has generally been given with the captions; for other images, efforts were made to discover the copyright owners, but without success; the author apologises if, as a result, any images have been reproduced without the necessary permission.

A shorter version of this study was published in *The Journal of Architecture*, Vol. 3, Summer 1998, pp. 85–105.

# I

# Albi Cathedral: design and purpose

IN THE MID AND LATER THIRTEENTH CENTURY the design of churches evolved new and disparate forms, changing, in a significant way, from the High Gothic architecture of northern central France, where the lofty nave within aisles, wrapped in curtain walls of glass, had been taken to what can be considered the limits of structural ability, and the perfection of an aesthetic and spiritual ideal. The tenor of religious life and practice was changing, and particularly as a result of the rapid spread of the Mendicant orders – Franciscans and Dominicans – whose missionary thrust, in rapidly growing towns and cities, involved preaching and teaching, a directing of their message towards the mass of the people. These orders thus required not a series of separate liturgical spaces, made dark by coloured glass, but rather (not unlike the Reformers and Counter-Reformers of several centuries later) a large, light, unified auditory space in which a preacher could be seen and heard by vast congregations.

While Italy and Germany developed individual versions of an open-spaced preaching church, the region of southern France and northern Spain evolved the system of building which frequently takes its name from Albi Cathedral (1282–1512). While Albi was not the first church created in this manner, it is the image of that building, as well as the means by which it was built and ordered, that inspired several generations of architects, churches, and unbuilt schemes, in Britain, from the mid-nineteenth century until recent times. The same region also developed another structural system for creating unsupported, wide-naved, open halls, using diaphragm arches: this technique, which is examined in a later chapter, was also employed in modern British church building, and evolved into a pervasive feature of modern architecture.

Fig. 1. Albi Cathedral, two recent views. Left: south side, apse and late Gothic porch. Right: north side and west tower. (Photograph (1988), Mary Kirk.)

The work of the Mendicants, particularly in southern France, was specifically aimed at countering the movement known as the Albigensian or Cathar heresy, against which Pope Innocent III launched a crusade (1208–18), and whose final extirpation was entrusted to a Dominican Inquisition in 1233, by Gregory IX. Likewise the Waldensian movement had attracted opposition and persecution from Innocent and Gregory in the same years, particularly in southern France and Spain, and Waldensian influence was also among the targets of the Mendicant preachers.

The Albigensian heresy takes its name from the city of Albi, which is built above a meander of the river Tarn (whose name is now given to the *department* in which it lies), some 40 km north-west of Toulouse. Abandoning the remains of a former building, a new cathedral, of Ste Cecile, at Albi, was built by Bernard de Castanet, the Dominican bishop who led the Inquisition in Languedoc. Appointed to the see in 1276, Bernard de

Fig. 2. Albi Cathedral, from the south.

Castanet quickly decided upon a new cathedral, but building did not commence until 1282;[1] the body of the church was completed to its original design in 1390 (Figs. 1, 2 & 3).

This building has been called the 'supreme expression of the huge Languedocian aisle-less nave' (Jean Bony).[2] Bony locates the experimentations of the new Gothic of the mid-thirteenth century onwards in three centres, namely Toulouse, Narbonne, and Barcelona in Catalonia, and Paul Frankl states that this Languedocian type of church, in which there are flanking chapels in place of nave aisles, was a product of the French Romanesque style, and strong local Classical tradition.[3]

The Dominican church of Santa Catalina, Barcelona (begun 1247) involved tall, rib-vaulted bays, with lateral chapels, set between the buttresses, opening onto the nave. The Franciscan church of the Cordeliers, Toulouse (c.1268–1305; destroyed in the nineteenth century) had a wide nave and buttresses, with low chapels set between the buttresses. On the (liturgical) northern side, the chapels are covered by lean-to roofs, and the buttresses rise above them, receding as they rise by means of stepped drip-mouldings. On the other side of the nave, however, the buttresses rise untapered, above the chapels, to full height, and a full-height outer wall closes the space, with a tall internal gallery-space over the chapels. It is this internalising of the buttresses, with the creation, in effect, of trans-verse* volumes along the sides of the wide nave, which was later to be developed at Albi and elsewhere.

---

*Most churches in western Europe are built along the longitudinal axis (i.e. the axis is liturgi-cally east-west, along the length of the church). Subsidiary volumes, spaces, and structures may be built at right-angles to that axis, on the transverse (north-south) axis. Thus the axis of a transverse vault runs north-south, as does the *plane* of a transverse arch, whose span therefore crosses all or part of the building, at right-angles to the primary longitudinal arcade.

Fig. 3. Albi Cathedral, illustrated in N. M. J. Chapuy, *Vues Pittoresques de la Cathedrale d'Albi* (1829). Note lack of parapet, etc. (Reproduced by permission of British Library.)

The Dominican church of the Jacobins, Toulouse (*c.*1275–92) kept the outer walls (and wide fenestration) on the inner-face of the buttresses, but bridged the buttresses just above the window apexes, at the base of a wide parapet, thus producing deep transverse arches, external to the building at that height, and also internally, below the principal windows, in the vaulting of the inter-buttress chapels. The Jacobin church, in addition, was a double-aisle, with a central row of full-height internal columns.

The Dominicans used double-aisles on many occasions, for example the Dominican nun's church at Imbach, Germany (1275). Both of the Toulouse churches have apsidal eastern terminations, in the normal French manner.

At Albi, begun as we have said in 1282, all the bays, on both sides (and in the apse), have a curtain wall running around them, linking the buttresses up to full height, and internalising the chapels. These were originally open to the vault, but a gallery, added above them in the fifteenth century, produces the effect seen in modern times (Fig. 4). The buttresses (above an outer vertical, then steeply-battered, lower stage, known as a *tallus* or *tallet*)[4] are, unusually, semi-circular in plan, on their outer-faces (Fig. 5); at their highest point, there runs a parapet, which, between the semicircles, is corbelled out on interlaced pointed arcadings, suggestive of machicolation. Between the buttress-projections, we can see the short, narrow windows of the chapels, and the longer (but still narrow) window-openings of the gallery-spaces, above. It is these longer windows, on the outer wall, which light the nave. Inside, the nave is a single space, uninterrupted by columns, with light entering obliquely from non-visible windows (at above-pavement level) via transverse volumes. At pavement level, the lateral arches open onto the dark spaces of flanking chapels.

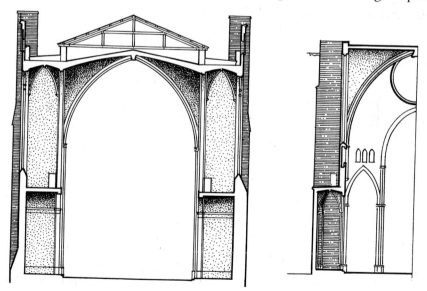

Fig. 4. Albi Cathedral (left) and Gerona Cathedral: sections illustrated in James H. Acland, *Medieval Structure: the Gothic Vault* (1972). (Reproduced by permission of the University of Toronto Press.)

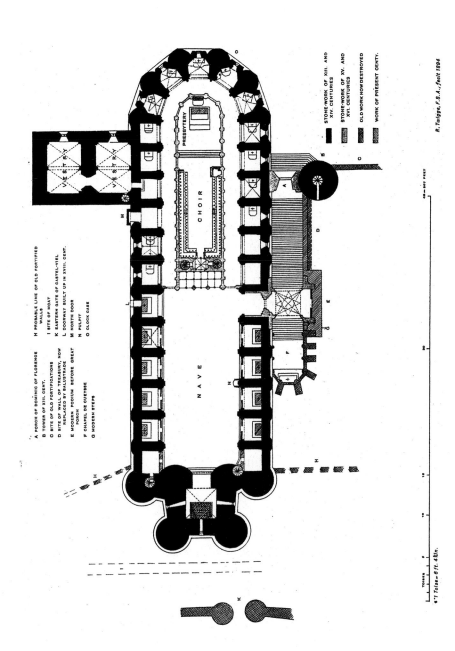

Fig. 5. Albi Cathedral, plan published by R. W. Twigge in *Archaeologia*,
Vol. 55, (1896).

Fig. 6. Apse of Albi Cathedral in the late-nineteenth century, from Eduard Corroyer, *Gothic Architecture* (1891, 1893).

These are rectangles in plan, whose shorter walls – that is, the buttresses – point north-south; the apsidal chapels are composed of irregular hexagons, whose outer face is the longer.

The parapet is of nineteenth-century construction. N. M. J. Chapuy's lithograph of the exterior (published 1829), shows the unfinished building as it was left at the end of the fourteenth century, the wall ending just above the apexes of the windows, a low roof seeming to slice the building off at that point (Fig. 3).[5] In the years 1844 to 1877, architectural journalist and building restorer Cesar Daly (1811–94) was the cathedral's state-appointed architect. Work began in 1850, there being extant indications of a machicolated gallery which may have been intended to rise above the walls. The parapet/roofline as created by Daly included turrets above each buttress at the apse (five are visible in Fig. 6, above, and in the photograph published in 1900 by Hubert Corlette;[6] only one is present today), and perhaps others in addition. This was later simplified, creating the present effect, with its essentially unbroken horizontal line.

The initial influence of Albi Cathedral was upon church building in Catalonia. Barcelona Cathedral (begun 1298) is in many ways a church planned on northern French lines, involving tiered inner volumes (on the model of Bourges); once again, however, the principal internal effect is that of a wide, uninterrupted space. The church of Sta Maria del Pi (1329–53), in the same city, also has a very wide nave and flanking chapels set between buttresses. At Gerona (also 'Girona'), a single-volume nave was added (from 1416) to an earlier aisled choir, the buttresses having pairs of chapels set between them (both an irregular hexagon in plan), albeit with the major windows, above the chapels, being set on the inner face of the buttresses (Figs. 4 & 9). The nave of Gerona is created by what are said to be the widest Gothic arches ever built (73 feet/22.25 m).[7]

Neither of these churches, however (nor later Spanish cathedrals, which featured wide naves and large internal spaces) in any sense drew on the overall visual effect and aesthetic characteristics of Albi Cathedral, which, it could be said, are not to be found, even in embryo, in those Toulouse churches which anticipated its structural system. Neither structural system, nor material (Albi, and also the Toulouse churches, were built of brick) are the source of Albi's appearance, which, like the Jacobin church, has the effect of an austere Gothic style (this is, of course, to ignore Albi's ornate Late Gothic additions: the north porch (1380) and internal screen (by 1512)). Albi's appearance is due to its function of defence.

As has often been said, in modern times, Albi was built as it was in order to be a fortress, in reality as well as appearance, and the choice of an internal-buttress system (although not new), not only produced a castle-like surrounding wall (with no flying buttresses, which could be easily pulled down), but prevented attackers from sheltering in the spaces produced by external projections (Fig. 5). The curious circular buttress-terminations (and massive, circular column-like buttresses at the angles of the tower), and also the deep bases (referred to) between the buttresses, all support this view of a church built in an unusual manner due to special requirements (Fig. 6). While hindsight shows the Cathar wars effectively to be concluded some decades before the cathedral was begun (and the heresy to have died out by the end of the century), such a conclusion was perhaps not apparent at the time. Frankl states that Bernard de Castanet was 'anxiously preoccupied with the need for defence',[8] and Kathryn M. Karrer sets the building's genesis in a volatile situation in which Bishop and people were engaged in constant struggle;[9] the defensive requirements of churches are known to have produced some perhaps curious-looking buildings, in southern France, for several centuries.[10]

# 2

# Initial published accounts of Albi

A LBI CATHEDRAL is perhaps a surprising church to be described in an early issue of *The Ecclesiologist* (viz. Vol. VI, No. 49, July 1846, pp. 98–101). So removed from the kind of church architecture that the early Ecclesiologists were intent on promoting, the (anonymous) author of this short article readily admits that the church could not be regarded as a model, and yet is at pains to show that Albi ('a legitimate piece of construction') demonstrates the appropriateness of the material (i.e. brick for building greater churches and cathedrals), and suggests that this 'may in more ways than one afford valuable hints for the future development of Christian architecture'.[11] Curiously, perhaps, the author suggests that the use of brick accounts for the semicircular terminations of the buttresses. The writer makes much of the building's uniqueness (i.e. in plan; he reproduces the plan from Chapuy's 1829 account (see Note 5), but no elevation or section), but does not exactly explain how the space and constructional system are as they are.

The influence of Continental architecture on British church building began to be felt a decade or so after this *Ecclesiologist* article, but increased interest in things across the Channel can be detected from soon after that time. In 1858, Thomas H. King, an English Catholic architect who worked in Bruges, published his four-volume *Study Book of Mediaeval Architecture*. This was a collection of drawings of buildings in France, Germany and the Low Countries. Four plates in volume one present the plan, cross-section, and exterior of 'Alby'.[12] Plates are also devoted to the Toulouse churches; the Cordeliers' church King saw as having internal buttresses, etc., on the northern side (only), because the church required defence specifically on that side. The brief text, set with the plates, is

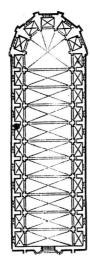
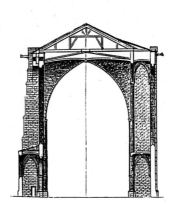

Fig. 7. The Cordeliers' Church, Toulouse; plan, section, and exterior perspective, from James Fergusson, *A History of Architecture in All Countries*, Vol. II, Bk II (1893), taken from Thomas King, *A Study Book of Mediaeval Architecture* (1858, etc.).

somewhat enlarged (in the sections concerning Albi) in a later edition of 1893. King's plates were subsequently used and reproduced by various writers in the nineteenth and twentieth centuries. One of the first beneficiaries of King's work was James Fergusson. There is a complex publishing history yet to be researched involving his *History of Architecture in All Countries* and the *Illustrated Handbook of Architecture*, but here suffice it to report that the (first?) 1855 edition of the *Illustrated Handbook* reproduces only Chapuy's plan of Albi (Vol. II, Ch. 2), likewise the second edition (1859); but the 1865 (first?) edition of the *History* uses King's plans and sections of the Cordeliers' church (Vol. I, Bk. II Ch. 2), and this continues in the second (1874) and third (1893) editions (Fig. 7). In the last of these, the text is somewhat enlarged, and the chapter as a whole presents a valuable historical account of southern French church architecture, describing and illustrating the churches at Perigeux, Souillac, Angouleme and Moissac, along with detailed descriptions of Albi and the Cordeliers' church.

A church which had been illustrated by Thomas King later appeared in a more popular work, the 1867 *An Encyclopaedia of Architecture, Historical, Theoretical, & Practical*, by Joseph Gwilt and Wyatt Papworth (Papworth's re-writing of Gwilt's 1842 work). This is the Dominican church, Gand (*sic*, i.e. Ghent; 1240–75) (p. 241), a plan and interior engraving taken, not from King, but from the *Gentleman's Magazine* of 1862 (Fig. 8). This church (which in his day, King tells us, had become a coal warehouse)[13] is a ten-bay hall with internal buttresses in the Albi manner; but unlike Albi and the Toulouse churches, it is square-ended at both east and west, and the (narrow) buttresses, rather than housing chapels, are pierced at ground level, to create a narrow corridor in place of aisles (there is no gallery sited half-way up the structure). The buttresses rise to form narrow transverse vaults, which (as King's illustrations show) are externally expressed as small gables. The location of this church shows that Dominican use of such a building was in no way limited to southern France. In September 1869, G. E. Street published *Some Account of Gothic Architecture in Spain*, the result of sketching tours in that country, a successor to his *Brick and Marble in the Middle Ages: Notes of a Tour in the North of Italy* (1855, 1874). This includes a plan of Gerona Cathedral, and an engraving of the interior; these illustrations show the wide nave leading to the aisled choir, and the flanking chapels set between wide transverse buttresses (Fig. 9).

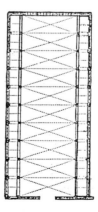

Fig. 8. Interior view and plan of the Dominican Church at Gand [Ghent] found on p. 241 of Joseph Gwilt's *An Encyclopaedia of Architecture*, new edition revised by Wyatt Papworth, 1867, from the *Gentleman's Magazine* of 1862.

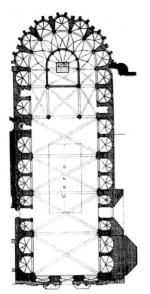

Fig. 9. Gerona Cathedral, plan and interior view, from G. E. Street, *Some Account of Gothic Architecture in Spain* (1869).

The inspiration of Albi and much other foreign precedent, in the High Victorian Gothic period, should not be a source of surprise, since it was not only Street who investigated Continental building types, and drew upon them in his work. Even architects whose work was not particularly eclectic, nor involved exotic elements, were interested in architecture abroad. There was the Foreign Architectural Book Society, which circulated books, (and probably drawings and photographs also), from its foundation (1859) until 1914.[14] This group included not only older architects, such as Street, Pearson (who joined in 1867), F. C. Penrose, Eastlake, Burges, Alfred Waterhouse, Devey and Nesfield, but also younger men, such as Belcher, Aston Webb, Lutyens, and Goodhart-Rendel; and we have seen that the Albi system of church design had established itself firmly with the *fin de siecle* generation of architects (though Sir Charles Nicholson, in an article published in 1914, claimed that 'the so-called 'passage aisle' plan is seldom a success' as generally 'the nave is so wide as to be squat in proportion').[15]

James Fergusson had noted (1893) the similar concerns, and architectural provision, of the Mendicants and the sixteenth-century Reformers. He writes (of the Cordeliers' church) 'there are few churches on the Continent which contain so many valuable suggestions for a Protestant place of worship, and no features that could not easily be improved by judicious handling. It was built in a country where Protestant feeling existed before the Reformation [a reference to the work of the Mendicants, no doubt, but surely also to the Waldensians, who should be regarded as 'Proto-Reformers'], and where consequently architects studied more how they could accommodate congregations than provide show-places for priests'.[16] The wide, uninterrupted-nave church was, from the late nineteenth century, to be used extensively for parish church and cathedral building, for the same liturgical reason, and not only by Protestants.

Published information concerning Albi was, by the end of the nineteenth century, becoming quite extensive. Not only was there the 1893 edition of King's *Study Book*, noted, but an English edition (1893) of Edouard Corroyer's *Gothic Architecture* (original edition, Paris, 1891). Corroyer's text (in addition to plan, section, exterior engraving, etc.) refers to the military character of the parapet's machicolation – but this is a description of the building as it currently appeared, of course, the parapet being new (Fig. 6). (See Note 6.) In 1896, antiquarian R. W. Twigge produced the most detailed study of Albi Cathedral yet published in English, drawing on a variety of French sources (e.g. Hippolyte Crozes's *Monographie de la Cathedrale de S. Cecile d'Albi* (1873) and an 1857 publication of Bernard de Boissonade's manuscript account of the church, of 1684).[17] Twigge published his own plan of the church, which was the first to give accurate information as to uses of internal spaces, and exterior structures (Fig. 5). Twigge's article was one of the sources cited by architect Hubert Corlette, in an article concerning Albi published in volume 8 of the *Architectural Review*, in 1900.[18] Corlette's account refers to the internal buttress arrangement – by then very widely understood and used – and his oblique photograph of the interior at the western end, showing the organ (p. 219), splendidly illustrates how the Albi system creates cascades of side-lighting, whose source is hidden. Another of Corlette's cited sources was Viollet le Duc's *Dictionnaire Raisonne de l'Architecture Francaise du XIe au XVIe Siècle* (1853–69). The *Dictionnaire Raisonne* was a mine of information on Albi and the Mendicant churches, the article *Cathedrale* reproducing a plan of 'Alby', that on *Architecture* reproducing a section of Albi, and that on *Brique* describing the Jacobin church at Toulouse. Corlette's 'honourably mentioned' submission to the first stage of the 1901–3 Liverpool Cathedral competition, however, was not influenced by Albi, but was designed in a conventional English Gothic manner.

Surprisingly, perhaps, the celebrated Bannister Fletcher history of architecture presents nothing more than a brief description of Albi (and the Cordeliers' church), until the 6th edition of 1921 (Albi's plan, p.460 F), only giving an exterior photograph in the 9th edition (1931). A 1921 *Architectural Review* article (which seems to reproduce exactly the same west-looking interior photograph that had been used by Corlette) was Henry M. Fletcher's 'South-western France and Albi', which contains photographs and sketches of churches at Albi, Souillac and Cahors, etc.[19]

# 3

# A new type of town church

ONE CENTRAL QUESTION, which occupied the attention of Victorian church architects, was that of the creation of a suitable plan, and form of building, appropriate to the needs of towns and large cities; the ideal town church – which would give large congregations uninterrupted view of the altar and pulpit – was a preoccupation of many architects, and various models were advocated.[20] In 1869, James Cubitt published a series of articles in *The Building News*, re-published in 1870 as *Church design for Congregations: its Development and Possibilities*. This, like the work of others, sought appropriate alternatives to the medieval plan, and included interest in wide-naved, aisle-less churches; the form and nature of Albi Cathedral and the southern French churches was perhaps a natural source of inspiration (Cubitt illustrated the plan of the Cordeliers' church, the plan of the chapel of the archbishop of Reims, and the plan and interior of the Ghent church).[21]

One church which was possibly the first, in Britain, to use wide buttressing, whose width accommodated aisle-passages (separated from the nave by a low, pavement-level, colonnade), with galleries above, was St Jude, Bethnal Green, London (1846), the work of Henry Clutton (1819–93). Unfortunately, St Jude's was badly damaged by war-time bombing, and today the only evidence of the church's appearance seems to exist in a few photographs taken for the National Monuments Record (Fig. 10).[22] While seemingly inspired by Albi Cathedral, St Jude's was unlike Albi in a variety of ways: not only did it have the pavement-level colonnade referred to, but it had a large transept, and principal nave windows which seem to have been set on the inside, rather than in an outer wall; the church was built in a restrained Round-Arched style. The

Fig. 10. St Jude, Bethnal Green, London (1846–) by Henry P. Clutton (1819–93). Interior showing barrel vault over tranverse arches, etc. (Photographed 1941, National Monuments Record; reproduced with permission of NMR.)

buttresses at St Jude's supported slender transverse arches, creating a timber, barrel-vaulted roof – and this is another innovative feature of this church which was to be developed in later decades.

A version of the aisle-passage arrangement, similar to that at Bethnal Green, and influential upon later planning, was seen in Street's All Saints', Clifton, Bristol (1864; also destroyed after bombing).[23] Here, deep arches, beneath the clerestory wall, are supported on pairs of short, fat columns, between which is a circulation space. The development of the aisle-passage, or narrow side-aisle corridor – produced by piercing the internal buttresses (as at Ghent), and giving them, perhaps, low-level arches – is the significant change which produces the British version of the Albi-like church.

A more complete and explicit use of the Albi arrangement was St Augustine, Kilburn, London. This was built by J. L. Pearson in the years 1871–c.1877, and seems to have been designed in 1870. In Pearson's characteristic Early English/Norman French Gothic style, the church has a vaulted nave supported by buttresses, beneath which are transverse arches; beyond the buttresses are further aisles, which are covered with lean-to roofs. Thus, the wide buttresses produce a double internal colonnade (at pavement level) above which is an Albi-like gallery (which, intentionally, created a separate seating space). At that level there are in effect two vertical structures, the colonnade which creates the nave, and another, further out, which creates the outer wall. Anthony Quiney therefore considers that Pearson used the 'Albi system' only above the level of the lower, inner, arcade; at pavement level, Albi's buttresses are not pierced by openings, because they house chapels between them.[24] Pearson certainly knew of Albi (his own photograph of the interior is reproduced by Quiney), but he also knew of various other medieval buildings which gave precedent for unconventional treatment of aisles and galleries. Quiney refers, also, to the inner aisles (with gallery over), and outer aisles, at St Barbara, Kutna Hora, Bohemia, but questions whether Pearson can have known of this church at the time.[25]

St Augustine, Pendlebury, Manchester, was built by G. F. Bodley and Thomas Garner in 1870–74 (Fig. 11). This church might be considered to be the supreme example of an Albi-inspired church in that it uses the internal buttress system (with transverse ribbed vaults joining the buttresses together at the apex of the nave arches), and yet also (unlike at Kilburn) creates a church which is pure rectangle, without projections, additional aisles, etc. (though a free-standing tower was planned, but not built). Bodley, when practising alone, had used internal buttresses as early

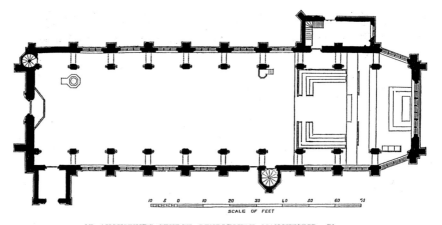

ST. AUGUSTINE'S CHURCH, PENDLEBURY, MANCHESTER.—*Plan.*

Fig. 11. Plan of St Augustine, Pendlebury, Manchester (G. F. Bodley) from *The Builder*, Vol. 35, 23 June 1877, p. 639.

as 1865 (St Salvador, Dundee). Churches composed of one single, rectangular volume, devoid of internal columns, had, of course, long been known to British architects, from English sources (e.g. the chapel of King's College, Cambridge (1446–1515); King's chapel, in the English manner, is square-ended, east and west, as is Pendlebury, though the sides of the final eastern bay are canted – the width of the buttress – inwards). The plan and constructional system of Pendlebury was still 'somewhat unusual', according to *The Builder*'s critic, of 23 June 1877.[26] Pendlebury's internal arrangement is unlike Albi in that the buttresses are pierced by arches, at ground level (side passages have emerged), and there is no gallery, or closing-off of inter-buttress space, beneath the vaults. Mark Collins considers that the use of internal buttresses, at Pendlebury, shows the last vestiges of Continental influence, which had strongly affected Bodley earlier in his career (and many others, at that time), but had been waning since 1865.[27] Bodley's assistant Henry Vaughan (1845–1917) (who collaborated with his Washington Cathedral scheme (1906–7)) built at least one church with internal buttresses among his many in the United States, the Church of the Mediator, Bronx, New York (1911).[28] William Burges' church of St Faith, Stoke Newington, London (1871–3; later completed by James Brooks; destroyed) had aisle-passages set beneath a high gallery, above which are wide, shallow, transverse arches, a use of the Albi plan which J. Mordaunt Crook considers Burges derived from St Jude, Bethnal Green (Figs. 12 & 13).[29]

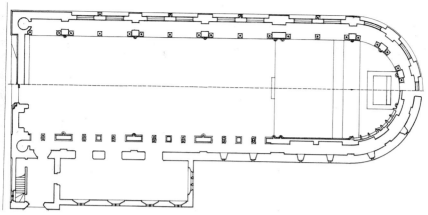

Fig. 12. St Faith, Stoke Newington, London (William Burges, 1871–3, etc.): half-plans at gallery and ground-floor level (reproduced with permission of National Monuments Record).

A use of the Albi system which (Andrew Saint seems to suggest) owes much to its designer's admiration of Bodley, was the first design for Holy Trinity, Latimer Road, London (Harrow Mission church), by Richard Norman Shaw (Fig. 14).[30] This scheme (from 1883) involved transverse arches, with passages beneath (recalling Street's at Clifton) set at each flank of the naves – naves, because Shaw first designed the church as a double-volume of vaulted naves supported on a central colonnade. As Saint points out, the unusual feature of Shaw's use of the Albi system (other than applying it to a double nave) is the fact that the outer walls, beneath the transverse vaults, had no windows in them (because of other properties abutting the church), and the architect intended to light the church entirely from large windows at east and west. (In 1886, however, the plan was changed radically to a large single volume, with external buttressing; the roof is a single, pointed, barrel-vault structure).

A particularly fascinating design is Shaw's (unexecuted) scheme for All Saints', Port Elizabeth, South Africa (early 1880s). This involved external buttresses, linked at the top by pointed (external) arches (which can be seen as short tranverse vaults).[31] This structural arrangement ultimately derives from the ancient practice of fortifying buildings by means of machicolation set on arches, which formed a high, external parapet, from which defenders were able to fire arrows at, or drop unpleasant substances on, attackers, through holes in the arches; this feature is known as *machicoulis sur arcs*. Machicolation derives from Roman fortifications and gateways, and can be found in the early eighth-century Islamic example of

Fig. 13. St Faith, Stoke Newington, London (William Burges, 1871–3, etc.). Interior after bomb-damage, showing deep transverse arches and aisle passages. (National Monuments Record, reproduced with kind permission of *The Architectural Review*.)

Fig. 14. Holy Trinity, Latimer Road, London (Harrow Mission Church), Richard Norman Shaw (1883–6). Exterior showing deep buttresses (photograph, 1956). (National Monuments Record; reproduced with kind permission of NMR.)

Umayyad Qasr al Hayr East; it may have travelled to western Europe by way of the Crusades, and other contacts with the Middle East. Various southern French churches, which were built for defence (twelfth century onwards) have *machicoulis sur arcs* (e.g. the cathedral of Agde, Saintes-Maries-de-la-Mer, Saint-Pons-de-Thomieres, and various ecclesiastical residential buildings and precincts);[32] this form is present at the Jacobin church, Toulouse, referred to above, and as noted, may have been intended for Albi. In the case of Shaw's scheme, however, the intended function was surely that of shading the windows from strong African sun, rather than anything to do with defence. (One product of *machicoulis sur arcs* was the application of arched pilasters to the outside of plain walls, creating the effect of tall, blind arcading (as seen at the west front of Agde); this was used by Sir Charles Nicholson and Hubert Corlette on the transepts they added to St Martin, Epsom, Surrey, in 1907.)[33]

Leonard Stokes was an architect who had worked with Street and Bodley, and in the years 1888–90 built St Agnes, Sefton Park, Liverpool. This Roman Catholic church could be seen as the first of many small parish churches, built on the internal buttress system, which were to be erected throughout Britain (in the Catholic and Anglican churches) in the first decades of the twentieth century. The spaces between the buttresses (at ground level) are simply corridors (with circular arches over this), and a gallery above, with transverse pointed arches above that. Stokes's architectural language is very much that of the Arts & Crafts movement, and the internal buttress system is regularly a feature of Arts & Crafts architecture.

If there was one serious attempt to produce a British church which was physically very similar to Albi Cathedral, it was F. C. Eden's plan for St Peter, Sharrow, the perspective of which is published in *The Builder*, 28 March 1903 (see Fig. 37, below). The walls, with semi-circular buttresses, high-set windows above blank wall, and the characteristic shape of the apse and its turrets, all appear very similar to the southern French work. The absence of a western tower (Eden supplies a tower of receding stages, characteristic of many of his designs, on the northern side of the volume) produces a square west termination, and the other feature which reclaims the English nature of the design is the steeply-pitched roof (and perhaps, also, the tracery). The six turrets at the apse – and other features of the drawing – have the effect of bringing Corroyer's engraving to mind – had Eden seen it, say, in its English publication of 1893? (see Note 6, and text below).[34]

# 4

# Half a century of cathedral design

## *Westminster Cathedral*

WESTMINSTER CATHEDRAL (a Roman Catholic building) was con-
ceived and designed by J. F. Bentley in the years 1894–5, and built
between 1895 and 1903. The style chosen (with the influence of Cardinal
Vaughan) was 'ItaloByzantine', and Bentley's main influences were the
Byzantine churches of north Italy (particularly San Vitale, Ravenna), and
Hagia Sophia, Istanbul (which Bentley knew only from an 1894 book, *The
Church of Sancta Sophia, Constantinople. A Study in Byzantine building*, by
W. R. Lethaby and Harold Swainson).[35]

While Westminster Cathedral, is, of course, essentially a Byzantine
building, it is possible to argue that it owes more to the nineteenth-
century tradition of Albi-inspired churches than has generally been
realised (Fig. 15). While the two ancient buildings whose inspiration
Bentley claimed are centrally-planned, Westminster is firmly axial in its
arrangement, in effect, a continuing series of Hagia Sophia-like domes,
supported (like those in Justinian's church) by internalised buttresses
('counterforts', in his terminology, from the French *contrefort*, 'buttress',
'abutment'). The lateral, or longitudinal, churches which Bentley saw in
his 1894 inspiration finding tour of Italy, included the Duomo, Florence,
and St Peter's, Rome, both of which he loathed.[36]

Bentley's planning requirements, 'both liturgical and congregational',
included 'a nave of generous breadth with an uninterrupted view of the
sanctuary to render it ideal for the reception of great multitudes on
ceremonial occasions...',[37] and hence the Albi-like wide, open nave. Albi-
like, as much as Byzantine, are the galleries, between buttresses, at 'first

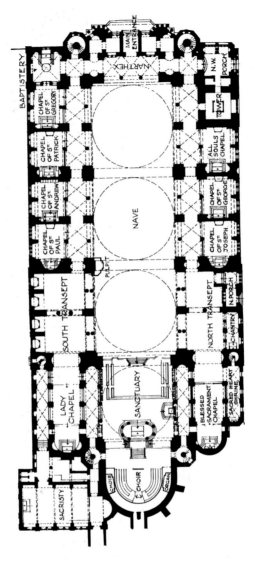

Fig. 15. Plan of Westminster Cathedral. The liturgical east is at the bottom of the plan.

floor' level, and also the wide transverse vaults which link the buttresses, and cover both outer chapels, and aisle-passages between.

Westminster Cathedral was the first great church in Britain in modern times to be built out of brick, just as Albi had been a major medieval example of a brick church.

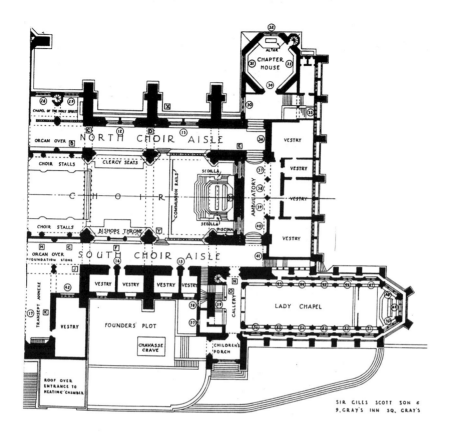

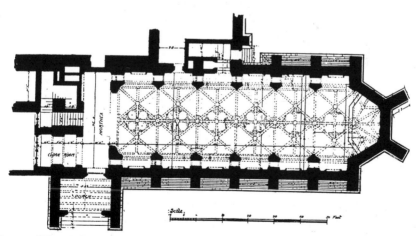

Fig. 16. Giles Gilbert Scott, plan of Liverpool Cathedral 'eastern' portion (above) and an (enlarged) plan of the Lady Chapel (below), showing aisle-passages cut through tranverse structure, in Choir and Lady Chapel.

## *The work of Giles Gilbert Scott*

In the second (1902–3) stage of the (second) Liverpool Cathedral competition (in which five architects were invited to submit schemes), the conditions set by the Building Committee involved a wide central space within the building, in which a large congregation could hear a preacher. The design selected by assessors Bodley and Shaw, that of Giles Gilbert Scott, did not have such a space, and at one stage it seems the committee were poised to reject all the entries and schemes.[38] Eventually, the committee approved the Scott design (a fact which caused further resentment, against the committee, by many architects and critics who were already angered by the way in which selection of a design had been conducted). The evolution and development of Scott's design, after its acceptance (which, due to his youth and inexperience, included a required acceptance of Bodley as joint architect), included, among many modifications, the creation of a central space at the mid-point of a very wide, lateral volume; and passage-aisles which are tunnelled through wide buttresses which support the principal vaults (causing the main walls, and windows, to be set on the outside) (Fig. 16). (These changes were introduced in the new plan of 1910, modified in 1924, 1927, etc.)[39]

The precise influence of Albi Cathedral, and other foreign buildings, upon Giles Gilbert Scott (1880–1960), is not easily ascertainable. Scott was clearly an architect who absorbed a vast range of architectural information and design sources, particularly in his early years. While he exhibited great originality and imagination in his Gothic design, both initially and throughout his career, such skill, as with any artist, comes also from precedent and tradition. While Scott quickly resented the influence of Bodley in the cathedral design, and reputedly had a low opinion of his master, Temple Moore, he clearly inherited a great deal from the late-Victorian Gothic tradition (though his early originality is shown at the church of the Annunciation, Bournemouth, 1905). The Liverpool Cathedral Lady Chapel (1904–10), in which Bodley had a design influence the extent of which is hard to determine, has narrow aisle passages cut through wide buttresses, which Collins refers to as being among various 'old Bodley mannerisms' present in the building.[40]

Scott, like so many architects before him, went on many sketching trips at home, kept a collection of photographs and drawings, and travelled and sketched abroad. Soon after his Liverpool Cathedral appointment, committee member and later chairman, Sir Frederick Radcliffe, took the

Fig. 17. Giles Gilbert Scott, Charterhouse School Chapel, 1922–7, exterior, from west (photograph, the author).

Fig 18. Giles Gilbert Scott, Charterhouse School Chapel, 1922–7, interior (photograph, the author).

young architect on various inspiration-finding excursions abroad, which included north Italy and Spain. Things seen in Italy (*c.*1908) probably influenced design of tombs and monuments, some fifteen or so years later,[41] and Spanish inspiration is much clearer, not only in certain specific items (the great central reredos, the screen of the Rankin porch), but also in the nature, and handling, of Scott's Gothic at Liverpool (Scott himself compared the size of his Liverpool vaults (72 feet/21.95 m across) with those of Gerona, which he appears to have seen).[42] But it may be that one of these early excursions included Albi, or that he had seen the 1903 F. C. Eden scheme for Sharrow (see above), for the clearest inspiration of Albi in Scott's work is seen in three sketches which seem to date from the years immediately before the First World War (see the Appendix).

Scott acknowledged his use of the internal buttress system at Liverpool Cathedral in 1953. In an interview with the editor of the *RIBA Journal*, published that year, the editor asks him about the building's structure ('aisles pierced through buttresses which reach to the main vault and thus avoid the need for flying buttresses and abolish the clerestory'); he calls this system 'unusual in buildings of Gothic form'. Scott replied that his motive for using such a system was 'to hide the aisle windows when looking down the centre of the cathedral, the intention being to get light without the eye being distracted by a large number of subsidiary bright areas...'.[43]

The buttresses at Liverpool are not (externally) concealed by any exterior curtain wall, and there was no attempt to produce any specifically Albi-like effect. In another work, however, Scott's design intentions were rather different. His war memorial chapel for Charterhouse School, Surrey (1922–7) is a single volume, rectangular in plan, other than an eastern termination resembling a domestic canted bay projection, between octagonal turrets (Figs. 17 & 18). Internally, the single-space chapel has large expanses of bare wall, broken by narrow light sources, windows discreet from internal sight. Externally, these windows are a series of flanking dwarf-transepts, expressed, above parapet-line, as gables. The eastern end, referred to, has something of the appearance of Albi's parapet.

A more subtle, pervasive, and thoroughly fascinating influence of Albi upon Scott has been suggested by the architect's son, Richard Gilbert Scott. A constant feature of Scott's work – be it churches and cathedrals in Gothic styles, or factories and power-stations composed of silver-grey brickwork – is the strong contrast and compartmentalisation of large areas of plain wall with smaller areas which, in one manner or another, are highly decorated. A particular example of this is the (unbuilt) 1942 western termination for Liverpool Cathedral. At Albi, the plain, unadorned, massive walls of the exterior contrast vividly with the later, ornately-decorated southern porch. The reason for this contrast of styles, at Albi, was, of course, the change of religious and architectural conditions in the intervening years. But it may be that Giles Scott was strongly influenced by this contrast, and, by some less-than-conscious processes, this contrast entered his own work.

## Guildford and Coventry Cathedrals: indirect lighting

In 1932, a competition was held for a cathedral for the new diocese of Guildford (created 1927). The winner, Edward Maufe, had set out to design a building which had pure cubic forms, unbroken straight lines, and a lack of decorative detail. Maufe considered that such a building (above all, its long, uniform, horizontal volume, and tower rising as a single mass, above the whole), was most appropriate to the site – set, as it was, along the length of a hill, outside the town – and was the kind of simple form found in Downland churches. Internally, Maufe intentionally created a wide, uninterrupted open nave, served by lateral passage-aisles, which are arched over at the height of the tall outer-windows, making the outer walls effectively a curtain around internal buttresses (Figs. 19 & 20). In the report (July 1932), supplied with his competition entry, Maufe claimed that 'a 'passage aisle' type plan for a Cathedral expresses modern requirements better than any other', because all congregants can see the altar.[44]

Maufe was clearly drawing on Albi, and his desire to create a wide, single space is shown by the use (in the guide-book he produced in 1966 for Pitkin Pictorials) of a diagram comparing a section of Lichfield ('here taken as a typical medieval cathedral') with one of Guildford (Fig. 21). The sections 'show that, though both cathedrals are of the same width and height... Guildford has a third more internal space'. In a typescript account, written in 1971, Maufe refers to his use of passage-aisles, and the raising of the aisle arches so that they share the point of springing with the arches of the nave (and hence remove the necessity for flying buttresses).[45] Guildford's aisles rise, not to full nave-height, but to shallow-pitched roofs, beside the nave structure – and thus, there is a low clerestory, with tiny windows. Maufe has used the main fenestration to light the nave from an indirect source, lower down, and contrasted this with the chancel, which is lit directly, light entering higher up; his aim, he

Fig.19. Edward Maufe, Guildford Cathedral, Surrey (1932–), interior (photograph, the author).

Fig. 20. Edward Maufe, Guildford Cathedral, Surrey (1932–), interior (photograph, the author).

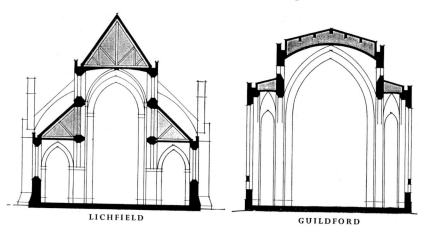

LICHFIELD         GUILDFORD

Fig. 21. Edward Maufe, sections through Guildford Cathedral (right) and a typical medieval cathedral (Lichfield, left) from the *Pitkin Pride of Britain Guide to Guildford Cathedral* (1966) (© Pitkin Guides Ltd., reproduced with kind permission).

explains, is to give a sense of symbolic/spiritual 'direction' from the nave towards a 'High Place'.[46] Also in the 1971 account, Maufe explains that when cost considerations had precluded construction in stone, he drew directly on Albi's example of a great church built in brick, and actually brought back a brick, from Albi, to be copied by the brick-makers of Stag Hill, where his church was created.

Maufe used the same ordering of spaces on a smaller scale at St Thomas, Hanwell (1933).[47] In that church, the aisle-passages are pierced only at lower level, giving a large expanse of internal buttress wall above. The

Fig. 22. All Saints', Darlaston, Staffordshire (Lavender, Twentyman & Percy, 1951), from *Sixty Post-war Churches*, Incorporated Church Building Society (n.d. [1956]). Reproduced with permission of ICBS.

Fig. 23. All Saints', Darlaston, Staffordshire (Lavender, Twentyman & Percy, 1951), from *Sixty Post-war Churches*, Incorporated Church Building Society (n.d. [1956]). Reproduced with permission of ICBS.

vault, at Hanwell, involves a folded-plate-like use of unribbed groin-vaults, contrasting with Guildford's use (in a way recalling, say, Charter-house School chapel) of strong, coupled, transverse arches. The same architect's All Saints', Thames Ditton (1938) sets the nave and aisle-passages beneath a single roof, which sweeps down over the whole.[48]

The internal buttress/aisle-passage scheme of church-building was also used when traditional styles were rejected in favour of modern forms, e.g. Lavender, Twentyman & Percy's All Saints', Darlaston, Staffordshire (1951). This is a large reinforced-concrete box-like structure, externally faced in brick, with stone details (Figs. 22 & 23). At each side of the nave are a series of tall, unadorned, concrete slabs, which support the shallow concrete shell roof; they are pierced at floor level, to create corridors.[49]

One appeal of the internal buttress system in the first few decades of the twentieth century, was, we have seen, its provision of indirect lighting. It is known that church architects at this time intentionally used restrained and controlled lighting in order to produce an appropriate atmosphere which was, in their view, conducive to worship and prayerfulness: what might be called a feeling of a spiritual place. Giles Scott (in a radio interview, transcript published in 1944) explicitly states that Liverpool Cathedral's 'essential quality of atmosphere', without which a cathedral

Fig. 24. Basil Spence's sketch of the porch of Albi Cathedral, from *Phoenix at Coventry* (1962).

Fig. 25. Sir Albert Richardson and E. A. Houfe, entry for the Coventry Cathedral competition (1951). Reproduced by permission of Simon Houfe (photograph from the collection of the University of Warwick History of Art Slide & Photograph Collection).

could not function properly, had been his 'main object to create'.[50] It is perhaps ironic, therefore, that architects used an internal buttress system (originally intended to produce a light, open, auditory space) to create the 'dim religious light' (Milton) recommended by such church architects as Ninian Comper early in the twentieth century.[51]

One scheme which seems to have made much use of indirect lighting is Giles Scott's 1945 plan for a re-built Coventry Cathedral (Scott was abortively appointed architect for a new cathedral, after the wartime destruction of the medieval building).[52] The interior perspective of this abandoned scheme shows light pouring down onto a central altar from non-visible windows which – not unlike those at Charterhouse School chapel – are set on the outside of the structure. Coventry Cathedral, in one scheme and another, provides several opportunities to observe the appeal of Albi, and see the way in which its inspiration took effect. Following Scott's resignation in 1947, a competition for a new design was held, in 1951. In his book *Phoenix at Coventry* (1962), architect Basil Spence describes his first visit to the site of the ruined Gothic church of St Michael (October 1950), and the way in which his vision of a new building quickly took root in his mind. He states that 'I was strongly influenced by the Cathedral at Albi, for although I visited this wonderful church in the South of France only after the competition, I already knew it well from plans and photographs'. His visit (September 1951) was in the period shortly after his competition success had been announced. In *Phoenix*, he describes the nature of Albi's appeal: the sheer walls of pink brick, the external rhythm created by the half-round buttresses, the emphasis on verticality produced by the narrow windows, etc., and the contrast of the plain exterior surfaces with the richness of the interior; 'If only Coventry could have some of that quality', he writes.[53] It is notable, perhaps, that the sketch of Albi reproduced in his book is not of the interior, or the sheer masses, but the southern porch (Fig. 24).[54]

By the 1950s, construction of large buildings no longer involved the traditional methods which had required buttresses, and, hence, the internal buttress/aisle passage structural system was a thing of the past; the Albi inspiration had by now taken other forms. Spence's fenestration at Coventry – alternating zigzags of wall and window – though arguably unlike medieval precedent in the south of France – was produced by his desire to control light. In his initial, anaesthetic-inspired, dream-vision of the interior (described in *Phoenix*, Chapter 3) the zigzag windows were invisible as the architect proceeded up the nave, but fully visible when he turned around; and he later used this zigzag effect to throw strong light on

Fig. 26. N. F. Cachemaille-Day, St Saviour, Eltham (1932–3) (photograph, the author).

the altar, from a non-visible source. Externally, the design made much use of large, plain surfaces of pink stone, and a vertical grid of fenestration. Spence's tall, open canopy of a 'western' porch (which rises over the height of the ancient walls, connecting new with old) seems to owe much to his sketch of the Albi porch, which emphasises the tall columns, and the high, open, inner space – and also the staircases which, as at Coventry, seem to spill out at various angles, from beneath the columns (though Gerona's west front has also been seen as a source for this).[55]

A completely different Albi inspiration comes in the form of the Coventry Cathedral competition entry by Sir Albert Richardson. Richardson had entered a 'sort of free Gothic' design for the Guildford Cathedral competition, but for Coventry turned to the solidity and massing of the great French cathedral (Fig. 25).[56] The architect's grandson and biographer, Simon Houfe, remembers going to Albi Cathedral with Richardson in 1959. However, although Mr Houfe has not so far been able to find documentary evidence amongst his grandfather's papers, he considers it likely that Richardson had previously been to Albi when travelling in that region in September 1921, September 1929, and 1935; certainly, during the visit of 1959, he told his grandson that he had been familiar with it for many years.[57] *The Art of Architecture*, which Richardson wrote with his former pupil Hector Corfiato (1938, 1946), reproduces a plan and elevation sketch of 'the fortress cathedral of Albi', and refers to chapels formed between internal buttresses.[58]

Richardson's Coventry scheme is perhaps the nearest we come to a cathedral drawing on the *appearance* of Albi. It makes much use of a grille of vertical features – slender, shallow buttresses; long, thin windows; sheer walls; and an overall cubic effect of pure forms (the terminations of the principal volume are severely flat and square). Having a single volume, plus a subsidiary volume set at a right-angle (the Chapel of Unity), the design has, in effect, the opportunity of producing two variations on the same theme. The thin windows of the principal volume are set beneath low segmental relieving arches, and the central 'east' window is sub-divided by two buttresses, in a motif which recalls turn-of-the-century Gothic practice (e.g. by Henry Wilson). The Chapel of Unity has a fretted parapet (unlike the principal volume, where we might have expected it), and its slit windows have sparse tracery.

Fig. 27. N. F. Cachemaille-Day, St Barnabas, Tuffley, Gloucester (1939) (photograph, the author).

Fig. 28. Proposed church and friary of St Francis, Dundee, 1933, Reginald Fairlie, from *Reginald Fairlie 1883–1952: a Scottish Architect*, by Patrick Nuttgens (1952).

This design, and particularly the Chapel of Unity volume, recalls a mode of church-building found in the 1930s, which, while evolved from Gothic, owed much to Continental traditions of Expressionist brickwork, as seen in some of the earlier churches of N. F. Cachemaille-Day. St Saviour, Eltham, London (Welch, Cachemaille-Day and Lander; 1932-3) is a concrete and brick box, with slit windows, thin strips of buttress, and a plain round stair-tower (Fig. 26).[59] The buttresses are not flat, however, but triangular, the nave being flanked by a series of sharp arrises. St Barnabas, Tuffley, Gloucester (1939) has the same cubic massing – and buttresses – but also has a fretted parapet (Fig. 27).[60] These buildings can seem to be Albi-inspired churches on a small scale (though the aisle-passages, at Eltham, are set in external, flat-roofed, structures, and countless churches, in the twentieth century, have aisle passages of this kind, i.e. not set within the thickness of the principal structure). A Scottish example of this style of church would have been Reginald Fairlie's proposed Friary church of St Francis, Dundee (1933) (and Louise Campbell suggests that Basil Spence knew of this design); here, the western termination employs two full-height octagonal columns which flank the west door (Fig. 28).[61] This style of architecture – vast rectangular block, articulated with triangular 'buttresses' – was seen at its largest and boldest in the Portslade power station, near Brighton, which Robert Atkinson built in the years 1946–52.

—◦◦◦—

As we have seen, the fascinating aspect of the influence of Albi in modern times is that it affected church builders and buildings in many different ways, at different times. In an age often said to be given to revival and reproduction, however, there seems to have been almost no attempt to recreate it, or anything looking like it (but perhaps one – see details of F. C. Eden's scheme, Fig. 37); and yet its various features (e.g. the structural system or the effect of the material) were often used, though only in part, or in a new way, in the changing circumstances, and situations, of modern church architecture.

# 5

## Churches using diaphragm arches

THE CREATION of wide, uninterrupted spaces by means of transverse arches, or diaphragm arches, is the other method of building, found in medieval southern France and northern Spain, which coincidentally was used extensively in modern church building in Britain. Early examples are the Cistercian dormitories of Poblet and Santes-Creus (the latter begun in 1191), and the church of Notre Dame de Lamourguier, Narbonne (c.1250–70).[62] The dormitory at Santes-Creus is a plain, single volume; the Narbonne church has its arches falling down onto short, transverse spaces (composed of pointed arches), which have a gallery above (i.e. similar to Albi). Both have roof timbers laid laterally over the arches, supporting the roof covering. A diaphragm arch is one which – unlike the great vaults at Albi and Gerona, etc. – requires no buttressing, the thrust being conveyed directly to the ground. This construction is said to originate in the Late Classical period, and to have been used in Islamic construction.

Construction of church roofs made of timber trusses and barrel-vaults (the latter perhaps employing strong transverse arches) had, of course, gone on throughout the medieval period, and been extensively re-used in modern times. In southern France, there were many churches composed of a single (stone) vault, running as a continuous arch, along the length of the building, perhaps supported by intermittent transverse arches, e.g. the cathedrals of Agde and Maguelone; the vault at Saint Pons-de-Thomieres is a pointed example. Each of these date from the twelfth century.[63] A late nineteenth-century British example of a (wooden) barrel vault, where the transverse arches are of stone, and set on corbels (and aisle-passages are incorporated into the plan) is St Mark, Mansfield, Nottinghamshire (Temple L. Moore; 1897).[64] A true diaphragm arch constructional system does not employ barrel vaults, but lateral roof timbers set, as we have seen, upon the shoulders of the arches.

Diaphragm arch construction of churches, in modern times, seems to have begun in the late nineteenth century. E. S. Prior built Holy Trinity, Bothenhampton, Devon, in the years 1884–9.[65] A specific intention was that the building facilitate the congregation's ability to see and hear the liturgy, and the architect produced a single, open volume – created by powerful diaphragm arches – as a response to this requirement. In 1886, however, the committee of the Incorporated Church Building Society, whose support for the project was necessary, reviewed the scheme. The committee (which included J. P. Seddon, James Brooks, Ewan Christian and J. Oldrid Scott) questioned the strength of Prior's proposed roof structure. A second committee, at the end of the same year, questioned the safety and economy of the scheme. In response to this criticism, the architect produced a list of English buildings of the thirteenth to fifteenth centuries, which employed stone transverse arches in place of trusses and purlins. These were: the treasury of Merton College, Oxford (*c.*1270); the hall of Conwy Castle; Mayfield Hall, Sussex; and the hall of Ightam Mote, Kent (*c.* 1310). Modern examples included the hall of Shaw's Adcote, Shropshire (1875–81). Adcote (like Prior's medieval precedents) was a domestic structure; its diaphragm arches, however, do not rise up to the apex of the hall, or close the space.[66] Among modern ecclesiastical work, which Prior cited, was Shaw's 'Willesden mission church', i.e. the Harrow Mission, Latimer Road (1885–6), referred to above. Here, however, the transverse structure is a wooden barrel vault.[67] Shaw, William White and David Brandon were members of the second committee. Prior agreed to strengthen the arches, and design buttresses, which project from the outer wall and rise up through the external roof covering. In January 1887, his plans were passed.

Prior's St Andrew, Roker, Sunderland (1904–7) uses similar arches, but here the roof itself is less steep than that at Bothenhampton, and the structure is not externally buttressed (except, once again, in the emergence of buttress-caps through the roof). A larger church (arch spans of

42 feet/12.80 m, compared to Bothenhampton's 29 feet/8.84 m), the arches at Roker are linked by deep arcading, and pierced through to form aisle-passages. Roker's structure is of reinforced concrete (faced with stone), a material which seems to have determined the shape of the arches; Prior's interest in this material came from reading Shaw's 1878 book on concrete cottage building.[68] (In the years 1901–2, W. R. Lethaby had built All Saints', Brockhampton, Herefordshire, which uses simple transverse arches of stone, above which was set a concrete roof.) Again, a requirement for the design at Roker was the congregation's ability to see and hear.[69] A design perhaps influenced by Prior's work is Arthur Bartlett's church at Dodford, near Kidderminster, Worcestershire (1907–8).[70] Here, as at Bothenhampton, diaphragm arches, supporting roof timbers, externally project through the roof.

The brick diaphragm arch was a major, indeed ubiquitous, feature of the work of the architect Dom Paul Bellot (1876–1944). Most of his works were designed for his order, the Order of Saint Benedict, and are to be found in Belgium and Holland. In the years 1907–14, however, he built the Benedictine abbey at Quarr, Isle of Wight, with its noble church in which the sanctuary is crowned with intersecting arches. Many of the abbey's conventual buildings (e.g. the refectory, chapter house and cloister) involve roofs laid – in some cases flat – over diaphragm arches; but the

Fig. 29. W. Curtis Green, St George, Waddon, Surrey (1932; screen, 1980s). A church created by diaphragm arches (photograph, the author).

Fig. 30. Holy Spirit, Harlescott, Shrewsbury (Herbert L. North & P. M. Padmore, 1936) from *New Churches Illustrated*, Incorporated Church Building Society (n.d. [1936]). Reproduced with permission of ICBS.

greatest of Quarr's diaphragm arch structures is the church's main volume, which is an enlarged monastic choir. Bellot was influenced by Dutch architecture, but also work in Spain which was Mozarabic, Mudejar, Romanesque and Gothic in nature. Paul Bellot studied Spanish architecture at first hand, probably in 1909.[71] At about the same time, the Spanish architect Antonio Gaudi (1852–1926) was drawing directly on the same local traditions (which included the arches at Poblet and Santes-Crues, referred to above).[72]

Diaphragm-arched structures became a very popular method of constructing churches, in Britain, in the first decades of the twentieth century. Giles Gilbert Scott's St Andrew, Luton (1931–2) develops the externally-expressed buttressing of the arches, such that they form wide, almost triangular structures, which flank the nave of the church.[73] W. Curtis Green's St George, Waddon, Croydon, Surrey (1933) fits the arches and their buttressing beneath long, low roofs, which sweep down beside transepts (Fig. 29);[74] a similar structure is the Holy Spirit, Harlescott, Shrewsbury (Fig. 30; Herbert L. North and P. M. Padmore; 1936).[75] A later work by Curtis Green (St Francis, Rough Close, Stoke on Trent; 1940) again used diaphragm arches beneath a low-sweeping roof, and used wide lateral arches to create open spaces in an eastern transept.[76]

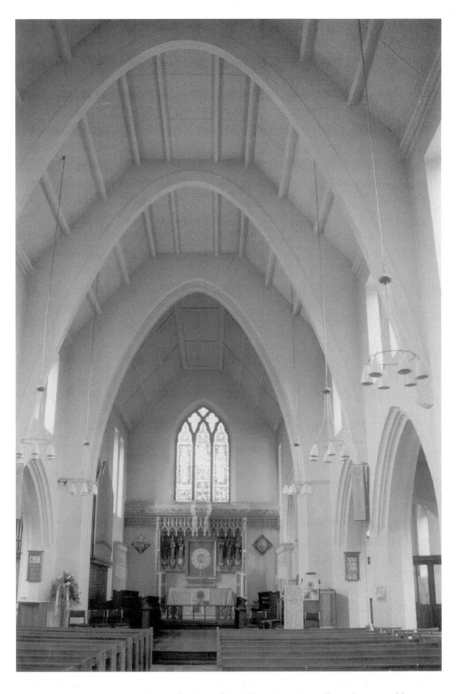

Fig. 31. D. Evelyn Nye, St Mark, Bromley, Kent (1953); a church created by concrete parabolic arches (photograph, the author).

Fig. 32. St Michael, New Marston, Oxford (Lawrence Dale, 1955) from *Sixty Post-war Churches*, Incorporated Church Building Society (n.d. [1956]). Reproduced with permission of ICBS.

Churches constructed of transverse arches were, from the building of Roker, the testing ground of new materials and structural systems, and this trend continued. H. S. Goodhart Rendel's St Wilfrid, Brighton (1933) employed tall, brick, fin-like columns (which rise through the roof) to support a structure of cranked steel beams.[77] At floor level, the brick columns were pierced to form aisle-passages; the profile of the ceiling, resulting from the nature of the beams, was one of three planes, the central one being horizontal.

One structural innovation which arose at this time was the development of parabolic arches (although British church-building did not produce the first use of these). These were likely to be of reinforced concrete, but the use of laminated (or layers of) timber was also developed. The arches could form a solid, parabolic roof above them, as for example at Bernard Miller's St Christopher, Norris Green, Liverpool, 1932, where the arches are steel-framed;[78] an earlier example, in Germany, is St Anthony, Ickern/Castrop-Rauxel, by Alfred Fischer, 1922–5.[79] Alternatively, the structure could be built out from the arches (perhaps at the point of laterally-set horizontal beams), to form window-spaces, aisle-passages, etc. This latter procedure is seen at St Faith, Lee on Solent, Hampshire (John Seely and Paul Paget; 1933); the arches here are of reinforced concrete. St Faith is fascinating in that its innovative structure, and resulting interior, is housed within a brick building derived from

Fig. 33. St Luke's Mission Church and Hall, Watford (Leslie T. Moore) from *Fifty Modern Churches*, Incorporated Church Building Society (n.d. [1947]). Reproduced with permission of ICBS.

Edwardian domestic classicism, and the windows that pierce the parabolic ceiling emerge as homely gabled dormers set in a low-pitched roof.[80] This building is an ecclesiastical interpretation of the kind of structure found in the spectacular New Horticultural Hall, built for the Royal Horticultural Society, in Westminster, in 1928 (Easton & Robertson).[81] Churches were produced in this manner for several decades, for example Lawrence Dale's St Michael, New Marston, Oxford of 1955 (Fig. 32).[82] A 1950s parabolic structure, within a 'conventional' Gothic church, is St Mark, Bromley, Kent (by D. Evelyn Nye & Partners; 1953), which is essentially a recon-struction after wartime damage (Fig. 31).[83] A similar church, by Jack Coia, is St Lawrence, Greenock, near Glasgow (1951). Here, the transverse arches are pointed, and shaped like vast Gothic lancets – similar, in fact, to the arches used by Maufe at Guildford (the passage-aisle arches are of like shape).[84]

The transverse arches have now become portal frames, standing alone. The frames at Welch & Lander's St Luke, Watford (1938; Fig. 33) are created out of five thicknesses of 2-inch timber; the roof laid over them is interrupted to produce a row of little eye-brow dormers, so lighting the space without recourse to the large dormers seen at Lee on Solent;[85] many churches, and other wide, open structures, have subsequently been produced from laminated timber arches and frames. Concrete portal frames, consisting of slender verticals and horizontal members, were used to create Cachemaille-Day's 1930s churches, referred to above, and there are many later examples of this kind – clear, open spaces, within a rectangular-sectioned box-like building. The continuing aesthetic appeal of strong arches, set against the principal axis of a space, is seen in Rafael

Moneo's Museum of Roman Art, Merrida, Spain (1980–5), which perhaps drew directly on local, ancient precedent.[86]

Plain, cubic buildings, with large, uninterrupted spaces and discreet lighting, are found everywhere within modern architecture, and it may be that in some measure the form and nature of which they are composed – and the structural systems which they are products of – evolved out of late nineteenth- and early twentieth-century church-building traditions, which themselves looked to late-medieval precedent in southern France and northern Spain.

# Appendix

## Albi on the Norfolk coast? Some curious sketches by Sir Giles Gilbert Scott

Giles Scott's knowledge of the 'Albi system' (the internal buttress church, perhaps with passage-aisles) would date from his first experiences of contemporary architecture, including the many late nineteenth-century churches of this kind which were produced in that phase of the Gothic Revival. Not only buildings, but many contemporary documents, as we have seen, gave information about Albi and other similar structures. By the time Scott came to use the Albi system at Liverpool, it had been assimilated in such a way that its structural principles were drawn upon in a subtle way, forming part of what was a distinct and original whole.

At about this time, however – the first decade of the twentieth century – Scott may have experienced/drawn upon the inspiration of Albi in a somewhat different manner. In one of the sixteen sketchbooks formerly kept at the British Architectural Library's Drawings Collection – book number 10 – there are three pages of sketches, which seem to depict parts of a church-like building, which have a very pronounced visual similarity to Albi Cathedral (Figs. 34 & 35).[87] The leaves of the book are 123 × 164 mm ($4^{13}/_{16}$ × $6^{7}/_{16}$ inches), a little over postcard size, and the first of the sheets (which are towards the end of those few in the book which were used) has a section, beside which is the exterior of an elevation, and above the elevation is what may be the plan of the outer wall, with plan-sections of two of the piers or columns. The next page shows an oblique view of an external elevation, plus various details of what may be the voussoirs of a rose window, and of corbelled masonry. The third sheet is principally devoted to an exterior elevation, which appears to be the termination of a volume, and most likely that of a west front (arches which seem to admit

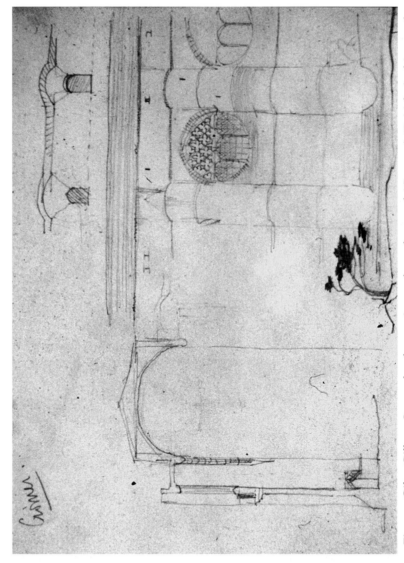

Fig. 34. Giles Gilbert Scott, sketch seeming to bear the word 'Cromer' (British Architectural Lirary, RIBA).

Fig. 35. Giles Gilbert Scott, sketch (British Architectural Library, RIBA).

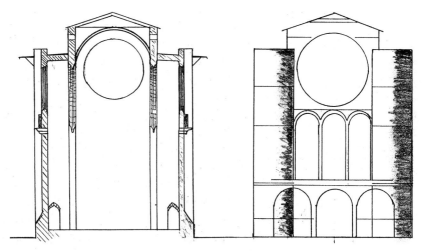

Fig. 36. Possible interpretation of the sketches by Giles Gilbert Scott seeming to bear the word 'Cromer' (drawings, the author).

entrance to the building are surmounted by a wide, three-light window, above which is a large round window, filled with mullions and Gothic tracery). This sheet also contains an additional sketch of window tracery, and an oblique sketch of a coping-detail. The first of these sheets has a written caption, at the top-left of the sketches, which seems to say 'Cromer'. The BAL's cataloguer has suggested that this book (which contains no date, or securely datable drawing) may date from '*c.*1912'.

The resemblance to Albi, which these sketches show, comes principally from the wide, curved, projections from the outer wall, which rise to the full height of that wall, and at base, die into a battered plinth or *tallus/tallet* (the buttresses and tallus, at Albi, as we have seen, are very similar). However, if the small sketch above the elevation is taken (as suggested) to be the plan, these are not in reality buttresses, but simply outer walls which curve outwards, preserving, as it were, the width of the aisle-passages, at that point where the bulk of the piers would otherwise make them narrower; externally, however, they appear as Albi-like buttresses (Fig. 36). The section shows precisely that kind of Albi-Gerona-Toulouse construction, which, as noted above, could have been seen in several contemporary English-language books, as well as in the original buildings themselves, and in various recent buildings in Britain. A small arched opening, just inside the outer walls, suggests that perhaps this was an opening pierced through actual transverse walls, so it may be that, above ground level, the bays are to be separated by transverse walls (or internal buttresses). While plain and solid, at their lower level, the outer walls are pierced at the higher stage by circular windows (which are indicated in the cross-section), and these are surely intended to light the central nave, light falling within the arches of the internal colonnade; these windows are perhaps the feature which is most unlike Albi.

The 'west front', as it appears, shows the final curve, or pseudo-buttress, being turned around 270 degrees to form corner towers, and flank the large 'west' window, with its circular light, set above three arches. In all of the circular windows, the tracery suggested resembles the reticulated patterns of late English Gothic, with quatrefoils set in ogival lozenges. The three arches at the base, which might be intended to form an outer porch, spring from the 'western-most' projection of the buttress-cylinders, or so it seems. These arches, and the loggia-like space they create, are perhaps recognisably part of the *fin de siècle* Gothic vocabulary, but the three-quarter circular corner towers, if they remind us of any-thing, recall the circular buttress-towers at the corners of Albi Cathedral's western tower (a difficulty with the design would have been altering the curve in order to make it fully circular, around the western facade, without being so large as to virtually fill the space between, making a large west window impossible; two tiny, faint lines, beneath the facade sketch, show Scott struggling with this problem, that of introducing a second, much-reduced radius, curve).

One faint, but recognisable detail, is found on the exterior elevation's left-hand pseudo-buttress: two faint lines suggest the possibility of the volume being terminated with a conical cap; this may remind us of the cones at the summit of the small towers or pinnacles which were added to the new parapet of Albi Cathedral in 1850–77. (In the late nineteenth- and early twentieth-century period – as seen, for example, in Hubert Cor-lette's article of 1900[88] – Albi's apse was known to have had five of these pinnacles, but today only one can be seen, at that part of the building). Scott used cones to crown the turrets of Liverpool Cathedral's 'east' front, though counterparts for the 'west' seem never to have been intended.

The 'west front' sketch, and the axonometric exterior elevation, seem to show extending drain pipes, intended presumably to throw out water from the aisle roofs, projecting from the pseudo-buttresses, at a height of roughly the apex of the circular windows; a very similar feature is found, at window-apex level, at Albi (and is shown (Fig. 6) in Edouard Corroyer's engraving published 1891/1893).[89]

What are these sketches? There seem to be two possibilities. Firstly, that Scott sketched part of a building, probably a church, which he saw in

Fig. 37. F. C. Eden's competition design for a church in Sharrow, from *The Builder*, Vol. 84, 28 March 1903.

southern France/northern Spain, or, secondly, that this is original work, and even the beginnings of an actual design for an eventual building. To attempt to decide which it may be, it is useful, firstly, to look at the nature and role of the sketchbooks. While most of them clearly date from early in the architect's career, the last two are much later (indeed, book 17 has sketches which are related to the post-1945 Bankside Power Station designs); it is tempting, therefore, to suggest that Scott used such books throughout his life. The earlier books are more disparate and varied in their contents, containing: sketches of buildings he visited, furniture, drawings of people (sometimes caricatures), notes for speeches, and even details of travel schedules and expenses (book 1 is his 1901–9 bank book). In addition, not surprisingly, there are those drawings which are related to the architect's ideas for parts of buildings he designed, and while some of these (as suggested) relate to known work (4 has an 'idea' for the eastern termination of Liverpool Cathedral), others seem less-recognisably Scott (e.g. a clutch of domestic designs – the only other drawings in book 10 – recalling Shaw and Lutyens). Number 6 ('*c*.1905'; BAL) tells an amusing story in which street urchins mistook G. F. Bodley (currently joint architect for Liverpool Cathedral) for Edward VII, Scott giving an explanatory gloss: 'Mr. Bodley somewhat resembles the King'.

The sketches of known buildings are records of Scott's early visits to churches in England (particularly books 3 and 4), and then of his journeys on the Continent. Evreux, Louvies and Chartres are found in book 4, and 7 takes us further afield: Florence, Venice, Torcello, and Genoa (University). A sketch in this book (which contains a sketch of the floor of Pisa Cathedral dated '28/9/08') is of Mino da Fiesole's Guigno tomb, at the Badia, Florence; my attempt to show that this sketch strongly influenced Scott's designs for the Earl of Derby memorial, and the war memorial altarpiece (both in Liverpool Cathedral), produced in the inter-war years, is cited in Note 41. These excursions were most likely those taken with Sir Frederick Radcliffe, a few years after Scott's success in the Liverpool Cathedral Competition (after 1902). It may well be that Scott visited Albi, in the first ten years or so, of the twentieth century, when travelling with Radcliffe, or on some other occasion.

A possible additional source or influence is F. C. Eden's design for a church at Sharrow, of 1903 (Fig. 37). As suggested in the main part of this study, the Sharrow church comes very near to being a building designed to appear like Albi; but a significant difference is the placing of the tower, not at the west end, but to the north of the building, and half-way between east and west. This meant that Eden's design had a 'west front' – and he has created it, like that in Scott's sketch, by turning the final buttress around three-quarters of a circle, and, as a result, making corner turrets, which project outside the line of the other buttresses; it is surely not impossible that Scott had seen the Eden Sharrow perspective in *The Builder* (28 March 1903).[90]

The possibility that the sketches relate to an actual building which Scott saw, and was determined to understand the structure of, cannot be completely ruled out. If he did see a French or Spanish church, it is surely one which would then have been called 'modern', i.e., later nineteenth-century. Contemporary French architects certainly looked to French Gothic precedence, though essentially of a 'northern' variety, the High Gothic of the Ile de France. In addition, however, some architects developed a strong respect for southern models, hence, for example, the influence of Perigeux, seen in the attenuated domes of Sacre Coeur, Paris (1875–7) (the actual exterior domes we now see at Perigeux date from the nineteenth century). An architect who particularly admired southern (and non-High Gothic) precedence was Leon Vaudoyer, whose cathedral of Marseilles (1852–93) is in what could be called a Romanesque/Italian/Moorish style.[91] A small town church, closely based on Albi, could well have been built, at this time, in the region. Certainly Scott experienced (saw, or imagined) a context for his sketches; they are not just something envisaged in isolation from reality, for the section/elevation page shows (bottom centre) what is surely a tree, bent over in strong wind (as occurs by the sea, or on high, flat hills). It may be, therefore, that Scott saw the building, and the tree, beside a Mediterranean shore, or on a mountainside. The inscription could refer to a place in France.

Alternatively, the sketches could relate to an actual scheme Scott had in mind. It can be argued that they do look like the first conceptions of an original building – the graphic products of the thinking-out of structure, spaces, and forms – rather than impressions of a building seen; and, despite the inspiration of Albi, the sketches would have produced a building whose nature would also have been that of an English church – the width of the bays are proportionally much greater than those at Albi, providing wide windows to admit the thin, northern light. If indeed the caption is 'Cromer', the town in Norfolk, this suggests that some ecclesiastical authority in that place, at this time, planned to build or enlarge a church. Early in his career, Scott principally worked for his own church, the Roman Catholic church (and his convent chapel at Harrow, and church of the Annunciation, Bournemouth, both 1905, were among his first products). Work for the Church of England only came later. The Anglican authorities at Liverpool had been somewhat surprised to find a young, totally inexperienced, Roman Catholic winning their cathedral competition, but after the completion of the Lady Chapel in 1910, Anglican work began to come his way, though most of his Anglican churches date from the 1920s/30s, and later. Anglican records (the Diocese of Norwich) have revealed no suggestion of major rebuilding/addition at Cromer at this time and no mention of Scott's name.[92]

If Scott was thinking about a church design for the town, in the first decade of the twentieth century, we must surely look for the context of this in the resurgence of Roman Catholicism in north-east Norfolk, in the turn-of-the-century period, recalled in a recent book, *The Catholic Revival in North Norfolk* (1995), by Charles A. Munkman.[93] In July 1894, Bishop

Riddell of Northampton (the area was in the Northampton diocese until 1976) bought a site for a mission in Cromer. A church, designed by G. Sherrin, was built, and completed in July 1895. It is a small (4 bay), low structure in a simple Gothic style, of the variety then used for garden suburbs. At the eastern end, there is a chancel arch – but, at that time, no chancel or sanctuary was built. In 1902, Fr Thomas Walmesley Carter was appointed priest at Cromer; it had been considered 'the most Protestant town in Europe', and only one Catholic lived in the parish at this time; the church, however, served many summer visitors, and Catholics from several hinterland villages.[94] Carter, lodging with his one parishioner, published an appeal in *The Tablet* (13 December 1902) for donations towards adding to the church, and building a presbytery.[95]

It is tempting, disregarding the proposed date of sketchbook 10, to suppose that Scott read this appeal, and began to think of a completion of the building, not knowing the nature, size, and proportions of the extant church (which is dedicated to Our Lady of Refuge). This is not possible, however, since Fr Carter's letter makes it quite clear that the church lacked a sanctuary, in particular, an area for the reservation of the sacrament, and Scott's sketch is surely that of a nave. Thanks to a significant donation, a suitable presbytery, stylistically matching the church, was opened in June 1904. At a later date, a shallow sanctuary was added (see interior photograph ('circa 1920') adjacent to pp. 26/7, of Munkman's book), and this was later (indeed, it may even have been in the middle decades of the twentieth century) replaced by a simple brick structure of one bay, which is extant. This sanctuary rises a few feet above the 1895 nave.

In 1902, the first mass had been said at Sheringham, a village five miles west, also on the coast. Fr Carter seems to have taken a strong interest in the mission to this village, and the result was the building of a church there. An account in *The Building News* (16 February 1912, p. 234) perhaps gives the impression that it was created in one phase; but the details reproduced in Munkman's book give a different picture. According to this, in April 1908, Bishop Keating officially approved the erection of a small church (probably on the specific recommendation of Fr Carter). In fact, the project must already have been well in hand, since the church was opened, we read, on 5 August; Giles Gilbert Scott was the architect.[96] It may be that Scott had been approached due to reports of his work at Liverpool (the well-advanced Lady Chapel), or his church at Bournemouth; but it is significant that on this occasion, the Catholics of Norfolk went to a London architect.

That the Sheringham mission was a success (large congregations, including many non-Catholics, attended the small church) probably accounts for the fact that on 1 September 1909, barely a year later, the bishop gave permission for the church to be extended; the completed church of St Joseph (again, designed by Scott) was consecrated on 2 August 1910. This slightly later building is a full-height volume set at right-angles to the original church and presbytery (which are set along Cromer Road). The first building was single-storey and barrel-vaulted; it was built on the same scale as the Cromer mission, but even smaller, seating a little over 40 worshippers. After 1910, this formed a side-chapel (also dedicated to St Joseph, who is depicted in the reredos-sculpture of what would briefly have been the sole altar). A later account than that of the *Building News* confirms this two-phase history (*The Architectural Review*, LXII, 368, July 1927, p. [lxxxii]), and notes that for the second phase a different builder was used. Fr Carter now became the priest at Sheringham (and as Canon Carter, he supervised Scott's further extension of the church – addition of two nave-bays, etc., and west front – in 1934).

However, the bishop's 1909 letter, approving the extension at Sheringham, included the idea of selling the site at Cromer to a 'religious institute of women', but 'provided another site, Church and Presbytery are secured out of the purchase money' (the large presbytery might have been suitable for such a purpose, the small church as their chapel). The Cromer church had originally been built slightly south of the town (as it then was) towards Overstrand; the matter of securing an appropriate site, in 1894, seems to have been a difficult one, which may have been somewhat due to the reputed Protestant leanings of the local community. So it may just be that, fifteen or so years on from the original scheme to establish a church in Cromer, the Catholic authorities sought a more central site, where an appropriately-sized church could be built. These plans came to nothing, however, and the only women's order to move to the town, a group of French nuns, bought a house on Park Road.[97]

It is fascinating to speculate that Carter had turned to Scott, with whom he had worked, and with whom he was to work again, for a new, larger church for the seaside town where his ministry had begun. This would date the sketches to about 1910. Perhaps, as had been true of the 1895 church, Scott had thought (or been led to think) in terms of a site near the shore, where the strong winds from the North Sea would bend the trees almost double (and many such trees are to be observed in the locality), where a tall building of powerful, original design would rise up to establish the standing of the Catholic faith in the local community, just as its model had, many centuries before, in the heresy-troubled regions of southern France. It is tantalising to wonder what kind of chancel/sanctuary Scott would have designed, for this church; perhaps the scheme was abandoned before he turned his mind to that problem.

It is perhaps tempting, also, to try to link the sketches with the designing of the Sheringham church itself, for this (or at least, the second phase) involved a large building of similar proportions to that suggested in the sketches, and the caption 'Cromer' could easily have referred to a place *near* Cromer, Cromer being the then-location of the client; but it is unlikely that Scott would ever have considered such a different form of building for an extension to what is a small, low building in the Gothic style he at that time employed, and it seems unlikely that Scott would have conceived of his Albi-like building when first approached for a small chapel at Sheringham.

# Notes & references

1   Alain Erlande-Brandenburg, *The Cathedral. The Social and Architectural Dynamics of Construction,* Cambridge University Press, 1994, p. 240.

2   Jean Bony, *French Gothic Architecture of the Twelfth and Thirteenth Centuries,* Berkeley/London, University of California Press, 1983, p. 451. See also Emile Mâle, *La Cathedrale d'Albi. Cent Trente et Une Photographies de Pierre Deviroy,* Paris, Paul Hartmann, 1950.

3   Paul Frankl, *Gothic Architecture,* Harmondsworth, Penguin, 1962, p. 141 (see also pp. 139–42).

4   Sheila Bonde, *Fortress-churches of Languedoc. Architecture, Religion and Conflict in the High Middle Ages,* Cambridge University Press, 1994, p. 46. James Stevens Curl gives additional variations of this term: *Encyclopaedia of Architectural Terms,* Donhead, 1992, p. 313.

5   N. M. J. Chapuy, *Vues Pittoresques de la Cathedrale d'Albi ...* (text: Alexandre du Mege), Paris, 1829, pl. 1.

6   See the entry under Daly in the *Macmillan Encyclopaedia of Architects,* ed. A. K. Placzek, 1982; see Corlette's article cited Note 18, p. 218. Information and contemporary illustrations of Albi were also published in Edouard Corroyer's *L'Architecture Gothique,* Paris, 1891 (pp. 101, 104, 105, 107, etc.), published in English in 1893 as *Gothic Architecture,* London, Seeley & Co., pp. 108, 111–15.

7   See the plan published by G. E. Street in *Some Account of Gothic Architecture in Spain,* 1869, opposite p. 338, Fig. 9, and the section published by James H. Acland, this volume, Fig. 4.

8   Frankl, work cited Note 3, p. 142.

9   'The Cathedral of Albi: an aesthetic choice or an historical imperative?', in *Apochrypha* (USA), 1, 1974, pp. 7–8.

10 See Sheila Bonde's book, cited Note 4, and Simon Cotton, 'The fortified churches of France', in *Church Building. The Magazine of Ecclesiastical Design*, 15, Summer 1990, pp. 4–5.

11 Page 100. Earlier interest in Continental architecture may have produced an account of Albi Cathedral, in English, before this *Ecclesiologist* article.

12 Plate 12, 1–4

13 1893 edition, Vol. II, see pl. 32.

14 British Architectural Library, RIBA (BAL), mss. FABS/1–19 and Jennifer Freeman, *W. D. Caroe and his Achievement*, Manchester University Press, 1990, p. 17.

15 Charles Nicholson and Charles Spooner, *Recent English Ecclesiastical Architecture*, London, Technical Journals, N.D. [1914], p. 9 [hereafter REEA].

16 *A History of Architecture in All Countries*, London, John Murray, 3rd. ed., 1893, Vol. II, Book III, Ch. II, p. 71.

17 R. W. Twigge, 'Notes on the Cathedral Church of St Cecily at Albi', *Archaeologia*, 1896, Vol. 55, pp. 93–112.

18 Hubert Corlette, 'Albi Cathedral', *The Architectural Review*, Vol 8, July–December 1900, pp. 209–20.

19 *The Architectural Review*, Vol 50, October 1921, pp. 75–83.

20 See Anthony Symondson's chapter (ch. 9, 'Theology, worship and the late Victorian church'), in *The Victorian Church and Society*, ed. Chris Brooks and Andrew Saint, Manchester University Press, 1995, particularly pp. 198–203.

21 See Geoffrey K. Brandwood, *Temple Moore. An Architect of the Late Gothic Revival*, Stamford, Paul Watkins, 1997, pp. 47–50, etc.; Cubitt's plate is illustrated as Fig. 7, p. 46. I am very grateful to Geoffrey Brandwood for many other suggestions, and pieces of information, towards the completion of this study.

22 See George MacHardy's unpublished thesis, *Henry Clutton (1819–93) and his Early Ecclesiastical Work*, MA, University of London, 1970, pp. 35ff. and pls. XI, XII, XIII (the photographs referred to in my text). I am very grateful to George MacHardy for making the results of his work available to me.

23 Stefan Muthesius, *The High Victorian Movement in Architecture 1850–70*, London, Routledge & Kegan Paul, 1972, pp. 134 and pl. 99 (p. 135).

24 See Anthony Quiney, *John Loughborough Pearson*, Yale University Press, 1979, pp. 110–13.

25 Quiney, work cited Note 24, p. 111.

26 *The Builder*, Vol. 35, 1877, p. 639.

27 David Mark Collins, *The Architecture of George Frederick Bodley 1827–1907 and Thomas Garner, 1839–1906*, PhD, University of Cambridge, 1992 (unpublished), p. 78.

28 William Morgan, *The Mighty Wall. The Architecture of Henry Vaughan*, Cambridge, Massachusetts and London, England, MIT Press, 1983, p. 72 (pl. 61).

29 J. Mordaunt Crook, *William Burges and the High Victorian Dream*, London, John Murray, 1981, pp. 218–9.

30 Andrew Saint, *Richard Norman Shaw*, New Haven and London, Yale University Press, 1976, pp. 288–9 (illus. 217, 218).

31 Saint, work cited Note 30, p. 287 (illus. 216)

32 Bonde, work cited Note 4, pp. 142–4, 160–71, etc.

33 REEA (Note 15), p. 8.

34 The plate is included with those at the end of the issue (28 March 1903, Vol. 84, No. 3138); notes on the scheme, p. 338. Sharrow is a district of Sheffield, and the *Buildings of England* guide for the area records only one church there, that of St Andrew, by J. B. Mitchell-Withers (1869).

35 See Winifride de L'Hôpital, *Westminster Cathedral and its Architect*, London, Hutchinson, N.D. [1919?], Vol. I, p. 35.

36 de L'Hôpital, work cited Note 35, pp. 29, 30.

37 de L'Hôpital, work cited Note 35, p. 37.

38 See Ch. 10, 'Liverpool Cathedral – A wholesome warning to architects', in Sarah Crewe, ed., *Visionary Spires*, London, Waterstone, 1986, particularly pp. 107–9; sadly, this book, concerned with original and neglected topics, lacks any references to the many articles, etc., it quotes from.

39 Vere E. Cotton, *The Book of Liverpool Cathedral*, Liverpool University Press, 1964, plans on pl. 8 and 9, pp. 21–37, etc.; also Peter Kennerley, *The Building of Liverpool Cathedral*, Carnegie Publishing, 1991.

40 Collins, thesis cited Note 27, p. 125. On Scott, see Gavin Stamp's article in the Grove *Dictionary of Art*, London Macmillan/New York, Grove, 1996, Vol. 28, pp. 280–82, and his article 'Giles Gilbert Scott: the problem of "Modernism"', *Architectural Design*, Vol. 49, number 10/11, 1979 ('Britain in the Thirties'), pp. 72–83.

41 John Thomas, 'Classical monument in a gothic church', *Transactions of the Historic Society of Lancashire and Cheshire*, Vol. 135, 1986, pp. 117–39 (concerned with the sources and evolution of the Liverpool Cathedral memorial to the sixteenth Earl of Derby, and other monuments in the building).

42 As Scott suggested in the interview with the editor of the *RIBA Journal*, published in the April 1953 issue, p. 224, col. 1 (see also text, below).

43 Interview cited Note 42, p. 221, col. 3.

44 BAL, RIBA, manuscripts: MaE/73/5.

45 BAL, RIBA, manuscripts: MaE/136/7 (information kindly supplied to me by Margaret Richardson).

46 Sir Edward Maufe, *Guildford Cathedral*, London, Pitkin Pictorials, 1966, p. 4, col. 3.

47 See Incorporated Church Building Society, *New Churches Illustrated ... Fifty-two Churches Erected during the Years 1923–1936*, 1936, pp. 36–9 [hereafter NCI].

48 See Incorporated Church Building Society, *Fifty Modern Churches ... Erected during the Years 1930–1945*, 1947, pp. 102–5 [hereafter FMC].

49 See Incorporated Church Building Society, *Sixty Post-War Churches*, 1956, p. 22 [hereafter SPWC].

50 'Forty years a-growing. A broadcast on the growth of Liverpool Anglican Cathedral', *The Builder*, 21 July 1944, p. 44, col. 2.

51 J. N[inian] Comper, *Of the Atmosphere of a Church*, London, Sheldon Press, 1947, especially section IV, pp. 26–9.

52 Louise Campbell, *Coventry Cathedral. Art and Architecture in Post-War Britain*, Oxford, Clarendon Press, 1996, pl. 15, p. 30 (and pages 22–31); John Thomas, *Coventry Cathedral*, London, Unwin Hyman, 1987, pp. 83–6.

53 Basil Spence, *Phoenix at Coventry. The Building of a Cathedral*, London, Geoffrey Bles, 1962, pp. 11–12, 26–7.

54 *Phoenix at Coventry* (Note 53), illus. 6.

55 Louise Campbell, work cited Note 52, p. 87.

56 See Simon Houfe, *Sir Albert Richardson, The Professor*, Luton, White Crescent Press, 1980, p. 187. His Coventry scheme is preserved in the Albert Richardson archive at the Bedfordshire Record Office.

57 Information contained in letters to me of 4 June 1990 and 21 February 1997.

58 Albert Richardson and Hector Corfiato, *The Art of Architecture*, London, Hodder & Stoughton, 1938, 1946, p. 78, illus. 60.

59 NCI (Note 47), pp. 114–7, and Louise Campbell, work cited Note 52, p. 85–6.

60 FMC (Note 48), pp. 118–9.

61 Campbell, p. 85, and see her source: Patrick Nuttgens, *Reginald Fairlie 1883–1952. A Scottish Architect*, Edinburgh, Oliver & Boyd, 1959, p. 10, pl. 29 (Fig. 28).

62 Jean Bony, work cited Note 2, pls. 278 and 279 (p. 307), pp. 448–9.

63 Sheila Bonde, work cited Note 4, pp. 74–7, 89–91, 99–100, etc.

64 REEA, pp. 58, 60, 61.

65 See Lynne Walker's unpublished thesis, *E. S. Prior, 1852–1932*, PhD, University of London, 1978, particularly pp. 321–33.

66 Andrew Saint, work cited Note 30, illus. 84, p. 101.

67 Andrew Saint, illus. 218, p. 288.

68 *Sketches for Cottages and other Buildings* ... published by Shaw with W. H. Lascelles.

69 Lynne Walker, thesis cited Note 65, p. 476. See also Trevor Garnham, *St Andrew's Church, Roker, Sunderland 1905*, London, Phaidon, 1996.

70 REEA, pp. 80–83.

71 See Peter Willis, *Dom Paul Bellot, Architect and Monk*, Newcastle upon Tyne, Elysium Press, 1996; and Charlotte Ellis, 'The abbey in exile', *The Architectural Review*, Vol. 202, No. 1206, August 1997, pp. 64–70 [Quarr Abbey].

72 See Thomas G. Beddall, 'Gaudi and Catalan Gothic', *Journal of the Society of Architectural Historians*, Vol. 34, I, pp. 48–59.

73 NCI, pp. 25–7.

74 NCI, pp. 14–16.

75 NCI, pp. 120–21.

76 FMC, pp 116–7.

77 NCI, pp. 7–10.

78 NCI, pp. 100–101.

79 Hugo Schnell, *Twentieth Century Church Architecture in Germany*, Munich and Zurich, Verlag Schnell & Steiner, 1974, pl. 70 (details: p. 51).

80 NCI, pp 76–7.

81 Dennis Sharp, *Twentieth Century Architecture. A visual history*, London, Lund Humphries, 1991, p. 88. A contemporary Eastern European example of a similar structure is Josef Kalous's Palace of Trade and Industry, at the Exhibition of Contemporary Culture, Brno, Hungary, 1926–8 (*East European Modernism. Architecture in Czechoslovakia, Hungary and Poland Between the Wars*, ed. Wojciech Lesnikowski, London, Thames & Hudson, 1996, p. 107 (3.62) and Frontispiece).

82 SPWC (Note 49), p. 20.

83 SPWC, p. 44.

84 See Robert W. K. C. Rogerson's *Jack Coia. His Life and Work*, privately published in Glasgow in 1986, pp. 38–9 (2 photographs). Andor Gomme kindly drew my attention to this church.

85 FMC, pp. 124–6.

86 Diane Ghirado, *Architecture after Modernism*, London, Thames & Hudson, 1996, illus. 45, p. 77.

87 Catalogue number: ScGG [187] 7 *c*.1912.

88 Corlette, article cited Note 18.

89 Edouard Corroyer, books cited Note 6.

90 See Note 26.

91 See Barry Bergdoll's *Leon Vaudoyer. Historicism in the Age of Industry*, Cambridge, Massachusetts/London, England, MIT Press, 1994, Ch. 8; p. 309, n. 37 (his admiration of Albi).

92 The archives of the Anglican Diocese of Norwich are now kept by Norfolk Record Office, Norwich. I am grateful to Jean Kennedy, County Archivist, (searches of faculty records, consistory court papers, etc.), who found no relevant references (her letter to me of 18 June 1996).

93 *The Catholic Revival in North Norfolk. Centenary of Our Lady of Refuge Church* in Cromer *1895–1995*, [1995]. Munkman compiled the book with the assistance of the present priest, Fr Peter Cansdale. Sadly, Mr. Munkman died soon after publication, and the checking of all his information has not been possible.

94 Quoted by Munkman, p. 21.

95 Munkman, pp. 26–7.

96 Munkman, p. 31.

97 Munkman, p. 25.

# The Ecclesiological Society

*The Ecclesiological Society is the society for all those who love churches. It was founded in 1879, acting as a successor to the Cambridge Camden Society of 1839. The Society has a lively programme, including lectures, an annual conference, and visits to range of locations in the UK. Members receive the Society's periodical,* Ecclesiology Today, *three times a year. From time to time the Society publishes monographs, of which this volume is an example.*

*Membership is open to all. For further details, see our website at www.ecclsoc.org, or write to us at the address on the reverse of the title page.*